SCHOOL LIBRARY SPACES

SCHOOL LIBRARY SPACES

JUST THE BASICS

Written and Illustrated by
Patricia A. Messner and Brenda S. Copeland

Just the Basics

 LIBRARIES UNLIMITED

AN IMPRINT OF ABC-CLIO, LLC
Santa Barbara, California • Denver, Colorado • Oxford, England

Library of Congress Cataloging-in-Publication Data

Messner, Patricia A.
  School library spaces : just the basics / written and illustrated by Patricia A. Messner and Brenda S. Copeland.
        p. cm. — (Just the basics)
  Includes bibliographical references and index.
    ISBN 978-1-59884-805-2 (pbk.: acid-free paper) —
    ISBN 978-1-59884-806-9 (ebook)   1. School libraries—United States—Administration.   2. School libraries—Employees—Training of—United States.   3. Student library assistants—Training of—United States.
  I. Copeland, Brenda S.   II. Title.
    Z675.S3M33395   2011
    025.1'978—dc22   2011002370

ISBN: 978-1-59884-805-2
EISBN: 978-1-59884-806-9

15   14   13   12   11   1   2   3   4   5

This book is also available on the World Wide Web as an eBook.
Visit www.abc-clio.com for details.

Libraries Unlimited
An Imprint of ABC-CLIO, LLC

ABC-CLIO, LLC
130 Cremona Drive, P.O. Box 1911
Santa Barbara, California 93116-1911

This book is printed on acid-free paper ∞

Manufactured in the United States of America

Dedicated to our library aides:
Lisa, Jean, Karen, Lynn, Peggy, Rita,
Sandy, and Thelma who have kept the libraries open and
us straight and made life easier in so many ways.

CONTENTS

SERIES FOREWORD

School libraries are places to read, to explore, and to find information. When kindergarten students first visit a school library, they are told that this is the place where they will learn the answers to their questions and that they will learn how to use the library to find those answers. And, as students grow and mature, the school library does indeed become that place for them, but we know that does not just happen. It takes a community, and that community is the library staff. The library staff must be knowledgeable, hardworking, and service oriented. They must possess a certain amount of basic information just to keep the library up and running.

Basic information is important information. It is often critical and in some cases not readily available. Running a school library well requires the assistance of several key individuals (library aides or clerks, volunteers, paraprofessionals, and technicians), in addition to the professional school librarian. Training these assistants to do the tasks required is time consuming, and often school librarians and district library coordinators have to construct their own training materials as well as do the one-on-one instruction at each library site.

In order to facilitate and help expedite this training, we offer this series of short, concise, and very practical books to aid in the training necessary to prepare assistants to help organize, equip, and furnish a media center; manage a school library; prepare and circulate materials; and perform many other tasks that are necessary to the smooth operation of a school library today. The Just the Basics series is written by professionally trained and certified building-level school librarians working currently in the field. As we roll out this series, please let us know what you think. Do we need additional topics? Is the series usable in training situations? What comments do you have?

Please contact me at scoatney@abc-clio.com.

SHARON COATNEY

Senior Acquisitions Editor
Libraries Unlimited
An Imprint of ABC-CLIO, LLC

INTRODUCTION

Welcome to a world of books, shelves, barcodes, and exciting adventures—a place where the imagination can run wild and new friends are discovered. Most library aides and librarians inherit a room full of books and shelves, a blank slate that needs to be jazzed up and organized. Others are fortunate enough to receive extra funds or wonder how to get started, where to look for supplies, and what to buy. What is done with the space is the key to a successful year. Start by making a list of what is available and of your dreams for what could happen. Organization is the kingpin. Spending a lot of money is not the key to success. School libraries have been working on a shoestring for years. In this day of budget cuts, we need to focus on what is working and what needs to be improved. Simple changes in arrangement of materials and supplies can create a more workable space. Books spread out and arranged in an interesting, eye-catching manner can entice more readers. Story corners decorated in joyful, happy themes can generate more positive comments for the library. Keep it simple, and make the library a happy place where staff and students want to congregate. Do not be afraid to ask for help from other professionals. Call in favors, visit other libraries, try a new idea, and read some new books. The library is the hub of any school, so make it radiate with energy and sunshine. This book has seven sections with information and resources to help a library aide or brand-new librarian set up a library. Good luck, and let the fun begin.

CHAPTER 1

Shelving and Book Arrangement

SHELVING UNITS

Most single-faced shelving units come in heights starting at 42 inches and going up to 84 inches. Easy or Everybody sections for younger students need to be the shorter shelves; the higher ones can be used for the fiction and nonfiction sections. Shelving for big books and special display shelving can be used if the library is big enough and space is not a problem. Various styles are available. Special story bins can also be used to highlight an author or special grouping of books. Arrange the shelving units so that outside wall space is taken up first. The freestanding shelves can be placed back to back to make them more stable and secure. Pay attention to the traffic patterns, as well. Special-needs students in wheelchairs will need space to maneuver. Shelving units that are free standing need ample space between them so that students can browse from both sides. These units also need to be angled so that staff can see all students as they browse for books. The library should be free of any blind spots where students can hide and cause problems. One librarian had round bus mirrors mounted at the back of the library so that students were visible at all times. The library had numerous blind spots, so this was an easy way to handle the problem. Shelving units need to be low enough for students to reach. For example: the Everybody/Easy section will need to be your lowest shelves because younger elementary students will be accessing these for book exchange. If shelves are too high to be reached easily, the top shelf can be used for stuffed animals, interesting toys, and special book displays. These can also be used to show off student projects that teachers often ask the library to house and display periodically throughout the school year. Shelving units come in several heights, examples: 30 inches, 36 inches, 48 inches, 60 inches, 72 inches, and 84 inches. Shelves need to be adjustable because of the various sizes of books. Everybody/Easy and Nonfiction books come in a wide range of sizes and shapes, so more space is needed between the shelves. Biography and Fiction are more uniform in size, and less space will be needed between these shelves. Book bins in the Everybody/Easy section can be used for grade reading levels, seasonal, or author sets, but bins take up quite a lot of floor space.

BOOKENDS

Bookends are needed for shelves that are partially filled. Magnetic bookends are great with metal shelves and are a breeze to use to help maintain order. There are also bookends that clamp on the bottom of the shelves. These are a little more complicated to use. Books should not be shelved so tightly that students find it hard to remove or replace a book. If purchasing bookends, always buy extra, because, as books circulate during the year, the shelves will empty and more bookends will be needed. Many libraries have a wide assortment of odds and ends. Sort them by what will hold heavy books versus easy picture books. Taller and heavier bookends work well with taller books, such as reference works. Try to see what is best for a section. Change them as needed and add bookends, as the shelves get sparse from usage. Some metal shelving units have shelf dividers or wire book supports in place of the separate bookends. These can be adjusted to fit the needs of the collection. If you are purchasing new shelves, this may be an option that you would like to consider. See the resource page for companies from which you can purchase bookends.

BOOK ARRANGEMENT

There are four major sections of books in the library: Easy or Everybody books, Fiction books, Biography books, and Nonfiction books. There are also sections that are not used as much, such as professional and reference books. Easy books are picture books with lots of pictures, not so many words, and pretend stories. Fiction books are chapter books, with lots of words, not very many pictures, and pretend stories. Biography books are books about real people. Nonfiction books are fact books that come in wide range of sizes and different levels of difficulty. Professional books are collections of teacher resources. Reference books are books that staff and students use for research.

Easy or Everybody Books

These books are arranged on the shelves in alphabetical order according to the author's last name. In the example E/CAR, the E means the Everybody or Easy section, and the letters underneath represent the author. Books can then be placed in order as needed on the shelf. So a book written by Eric Carle would appear on the shelf before a book written by Denys Cazet. CAR would come before CAZ in alphabetical order. Special stickers can be placed on the spine to identify holiday books, Caldecott Award winners, books on animals, and so on. See companies on the resource page.

Fiction Books

Books in this section have either F or FIC on the spine label, with the first three letters of the author's name underneath. They are then placed in alphabetical order. Some libraries pull a group or series of books and display them on a separate shelf. For example, Choose Your Own Adventures might be on a shelf at the end of the fiction section. These books might all have different authors but are asked for a lot on the elementary level. Pulling a group or series of books usually is determined by the staff and sometimes helps to highlight a grouping. Students are drawn to them, and circulation will increase. Spine or classification labels can be purchased at DEMCO or The Library Store; see the resource page. These stickers make browsing for book favorites easier. They are attached above the call number when possible. Peel the label from roll, attach it to the spine, and add a clear label plastic strip over the top for longer wear. Start off with most frequently asked-for categories, such as cats, horses, dogs, Caldecott and Newbery winners, and mysteries. Others can be added as the need warrants. Some libraries label easy-reader picture books with a colored dot. These books have fewer words to a page. At the beginning of the year, students just learning to read will ask for these.

Biographies

These are kept all together in a separate grouping. They are arranged on the shelf and labeled with 92 or B on the spine. Underneath that number are the first three letters of the name of the subject of the book. So 92/WAS or B/WAS would be the call number for Washington, and 92/ADA or B/ADA would be the call number for Adams. Again they are shelved in alphabetical order according to the person's name. All other sections of the library are placed on the shelf by the author's last name. Individual biographies are placed on the shelves first. The collective biographies come after that and are arranged by the author's last name, for example, 920/ADL.

Nonfiction—The Dewey Decimal System

Fact books all have a number on the spine. This is called the call number because at one time, library patrons were not allowed to go into the stacks to get their own materials, so they looked up the number of the book in the card catalog and "called it out" to a library staff person, who then retrieved the book for the patron. The call numbers are the method used so that all of the same kind of book have a same or similar number on the spine and are shelved together. Melville Dewey designed this system, and it continues to be used in libraries after more than 100 years. For example, all dog books have the number 636.7. Each book has the first three letters of the author's name under that number. All dog books are located side by side on the shelf in alphabetical order according to the author's name. The pet category is 636. The number after the decimal point tells which kind of pet book it is. There are 10 categories in the nonfiction section.

000 General books: encyclopedias, computer books
100 Emotions, feelings, supernatural events
200 Religion
300 Social Science
400 Languages
500 Science and all related fields, including animals
600 Technology, pets, human body
700 Sports and recreation
800 Literature
900 History and geography

Reference

Reference books have a Dewey number, but above the Dewey number are the letters REF. REF stands for the reference section. These books do not usually circulate and need to be shelved by themselves. Some libraries let these books be checked out by a classroom teacher for a short amount of time.

Professional

Professional books are located in a back room or off the beaten path. Call numbers are usually Dewey numbers with P or Pro above the number.

SHELVING BOOKS

Older elementary students do a good job of helping to shelve books. Some libraries allow a selected group of students to miss one recess a week to help in the library. This requires some good training on the part of library staff at the beginning of the year, but it pays off as the year gets busier. It is usually better to start students off with the Everybody/Easy books and then let them move up to Fiction and Nonfiction as they get more confident in their work. Having a few students at a time works better than having a whole crew. Pick students that are dependable, and it is great to select students who do not get to do other things at school. Even students with academic challenges enjoy putting books away, and they can prove to be some of the best workers.

Train students to shelve the books so that they sit on the edge of each shelf, as this makes it easier for patrons to read the spines of the books as they browse the library. Also, the flow of the shelves follows a zigzag pattern. Students should begin in the top left corner and proceed across the shelf to the divider. When the students reach the divider, they should go down to the next shelf. In other words, if there are several shelving units next to each other, the books are shelved within the individual shelving units, filling up one whole shelving unit before going to the next unit. They are not shelved across shelving units. See the shelf graph for the flow of shelves.

Parent volunteers are wonderful to tap for maintaining shelves. A fixed schedule of time for parents works better. Mix parents who have shelved in the past years with newcomers. They will be able to help and maintain the collection in better order. See the sample parent letter that can be sent home at the beginning of the year. Volunteers are wonderful but sometimes things happen and they don't show up because of various reasons and the staff is left with the job of shelving books.

The third way to maintain shelves is for the library staff to do the work themselves. The one advantage of this is that the library staff can readily see damaged books and sections of the library that need to be updated when funds become available. Staff can easily spot favorites and trends in student reading. When teachers ask for classroom collections, staff can find what is needed because they have handled the collection enough to know what age-appropriate levels are needed. The staff will be overseeing the shelving of the books, and on lots of occasions they will help the volunteers complete the great task of shelving the books. Probably the easiest way to keep the collection current is once a month to take a section of the library and check for damaged books that need mending and also for old materials that might need to be weeded out. Lots of times, they can be spotted by just looking at the covers. Student favorites show a lot of wear. Copyright dates can be checked if necessary. Books with black-and-white pictures are easy to spot when flipping through the pages. Some teachers ask for the same collections each year, and it is helpful to have a list of these that can be pulled out to save time. Keep a binder, file folder, or a list on the computer with teacher request lists.

SHELF READING

Shelf reading is checking the shelves for misfiled books and is a job that needs to be done continually. Depending on the number of volunteers and staff, shelf reading can be completed on a rotating schedule, maybe once every two weeks. The library staff can be inserted into the rotating schedule on the days when there are not as many classes and the staff has more flexible time. See the example of a sample schedule.

SHELVING AND BOOK ARRANGEMENT

Shelf Reading Schedule

SECTIONS	DAY 1	DAY 2	DAY 3	DAY 4	DAY 5	DAY 4	DAY 7	DAY 8	DAY 9	DAY 10
Everybody/ Easy										
A-G										
H-M										
N-R										
S-Z										
Fiction										
A-G										
H-M										
N-R										
S-Z										
Nonfiction										
000-299										
300-399										
400-599										
600-699										
700-799										
800-999										
Biography										
A-G										
H-M										
N-R										
S-Z										

SHELVING AND BOOK ARRANGEMENT

Shelf Graph

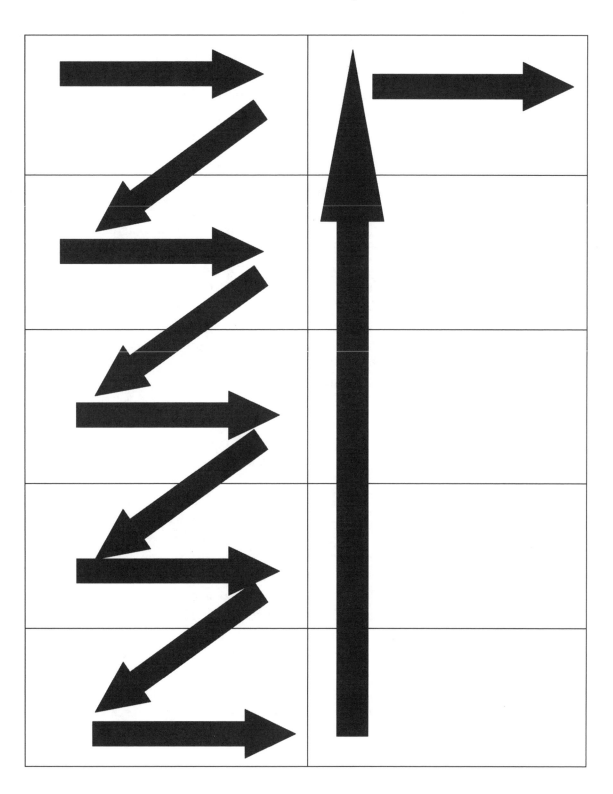

CARTS FOR SHELVING BOOKS

Carts are needed for returned books. Check books in and place them on the cart. One way is to take the cart and divide the shelves on the cart into the four different kinds of books in the library (Easy or Everybody Books, Fiction, Biography, and Nonfiction). Arrange the books on the cart in ABC order by the author's last name for the Easy, Fiction, and Biography sections and in number order for the Nonfiction books. After all the books are checked in and arranged on the cart, take the cart out to the shelves and put the books in order by interfiling them with books already on the correct shelves. If there are no carts available, place books on the top shelves in the correct section close to the location for the books. After all the books are checked in, then the staff can go back to the shelves and put the books in order on the correct shelves.

Second, if space and money are available to acquire more than one cart, students can sort the books by placing them on the correctly labeled cart as part of the checking-in process. See following sample cart labels at the end of this chapter. It is best to have each cart be a different color. When you are giving directions, students can make the connection if you tell them to place the books on the red Everybody cart. After books have been checked in, students can be trained to page through the books to see if any repairs are needed. Also, check for loose spines by grasping the front and back cover with both hands; if the spine is pulled away from the pages, then lay the book aside for repairs. Student helpers or parent volunteers can then take the carts to the correct sections and put the books back on the shelves. Periodically during the day, staff should take time to remove books from the cart. Either place the books on top for shelving later, or shelve books on the go. This will help keep the carts less messy and make housekeeping easier. If carts become too full, then students start stacking them in all directions. It is good to get the books back on the shelves as soon as possible for recirculation.

At the beginning of the year, it is best to select a policeman for each category. Rotate each week with a different crew. After books are checked in, students must show the policeman the call number. If it matches the cart or category that the student is covering, the policeman says "Green light." If it is incorrect, the policeman says "Red light." Make up a sample of each category and laminate it. The policeman can show what the call number should look like. Later in the year, the crew of policemen can become smaller as the students learn what each category is and on which cart the books belong.

Parents, students, and community members make great volunteer help for the library. Sending out letters to parents, advertising in teacher newsletters, and posting on school websites are all possible ways to get help for the library. Have students fill out an application for the position of student volunteer. Students who make the effort to fill out the application really want to help in the library. See the sample parent letter and student application. Gathering the volunteers together for a training session and orientation is a good way to show off the library and to explain the positions that are available. Volunteers can see the schedule, and, working together, they can fill the slots. Serving cookies and drinks always brings people in, so make this a part of the training.

SHELVING AND BOOK ARRANGEMENT

Volunteer Letter

PARENT VOLUNTEERS

Dear Parent,

The library is in need of parents to shelve books and help with projects throughout the coming school year. Volunteers can be a big help during the school day. It would be most helpful if you could commit to a set time period every week. Even half an hour can be a big help. If you can volunteer, please fill in the information at the bottom of the paper and return it to the library. Thanks in advance for all your help.

Sincerely,

_____

✂ -

Name:_____

Phone number_____

AM _____   PM _____

Monday_____ Tuesday _____ Wednesday_____

Thursday_____ Friday_____

I can only help on occasion when I have free time. I would be willing to be on a call list for those times.   Yes_____

The only time I could help   _____

SHELVING AND BOOK ARRANGEMENT

Student Application

STUDENT VOLUNTEER APPLICATION

I would be willing to give up one recess a week to work in the library because

_____

_____

Your Name_____

Parent's or Guardian Signature_____

Teacher's Signature_____

Room Number_____

Positions that I am interested in:

_____ Shelf reading _____Shelving books _____Dusting

_____Organizing supplies _____Helping younger students select books

*Please note that both your classroom teacher and your parent or guardian must sign this form in order for you to be chosen for this position.

From *School Library Spaces: Just the Basics* by Patricia A. Messner and Brenda S. Copeland. Santa Barbara, CA: Libraries Unlimited. Copyright © 2011.

SHELVING AND BOOK ARRANGEMENT

Cart Signs

Everybody/Easy
Cart

Fiction
Cart

Nonfiction
Cart

E **BRO**	**B** **LIN**
398.2 **GIB**	**92** **LIN**

Call Numbers

920 **BRO**	**F** **ANT**
FIC **ANT**	**REF** **398.2** **GIB**

SHELVING AND BOOK ARRANGEMENT

Call Numbers

PRO
398
BRO

RESOURCES

Brodart Supplies & Furnishings
100 North Road, P.O. Box 300
McElhattan, PA 17748
www.shopbrodart.com

DEMCO
P.O. Box 7488
Madison, WI 53707-7488
www.demco.com

Gaylord Bros.
P.O. Box 4901
Syracuse, NY 13221-4901
www.gaylord.com

The Library Store, Inc.
P.O. Box 0964
112 E. South Street
Tremont, IL 61568-0964
www.thelibrarystore.com

CHAPTER 2

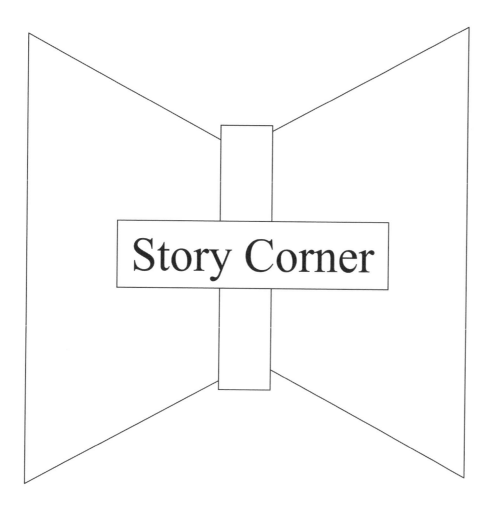

The story corner is one of the busiest places in any elementary school library. Younger classes meet here each week for story time, and older students find it a cool place to hang out with a favorite book. Students will soon learn that adventure awaits them when they arrive for story time. The library staff will need to make this area a fun place but one that is conducive to quiet reading as well as dramatic storytelling times. The space needs to be large enough so that a class of elementary students can sit comfortably on the floor. Sometimes a space off by itself works best, especially if the library is a high-traffic area with staff and students dropping in throughout the day. Look around for the best place, and transform it into an adventure zone.

LOCATION

The size of the library will determine the best location for the story corner. For a small library about the size of a regular classroom, the story corner might be located near the Everybody/Easy books and out of high-traffic areas. An area clear of tables and chairs is needed so that a class of students can sit on the floor. If there is not enough room near the Everybody/Easy books, the middle of the room will work. A story pit is ideal and usually built into the floor. There are steps going down with an elevated seating area that can be used for several classrooms of students. It doesn't matter where the story corner is located; just make it a special place with few distractions. The diagrams of story corners offer some suggested layouts.

STORY CORNER

Everybody/Easy Location

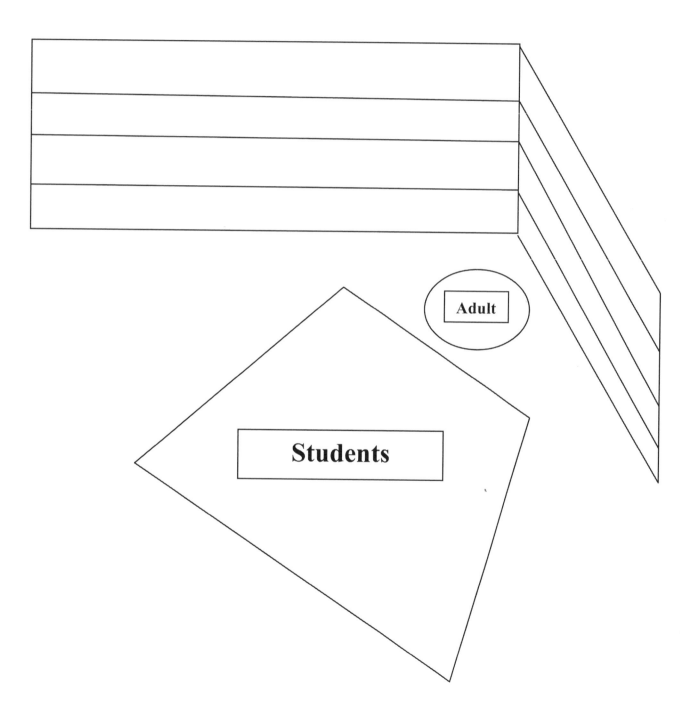

Everybody/Easy Books

Adult

Students

STORY CORNER

Middle-of-the-Room Location

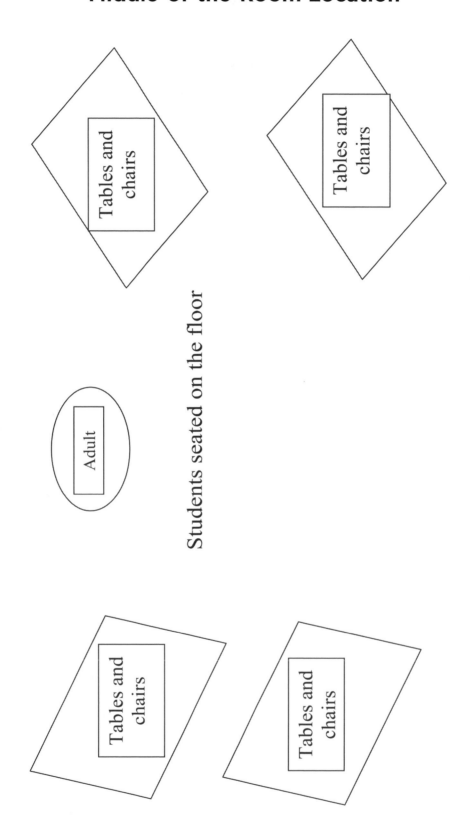

From *School Library Spaces: Just the Basics* by Patricia A. Messner and Brenda S. Copeland. Santa Barbara, CA: Libraries Unlimited. Copyright © 2011.

STORY CORNER

Story Pit

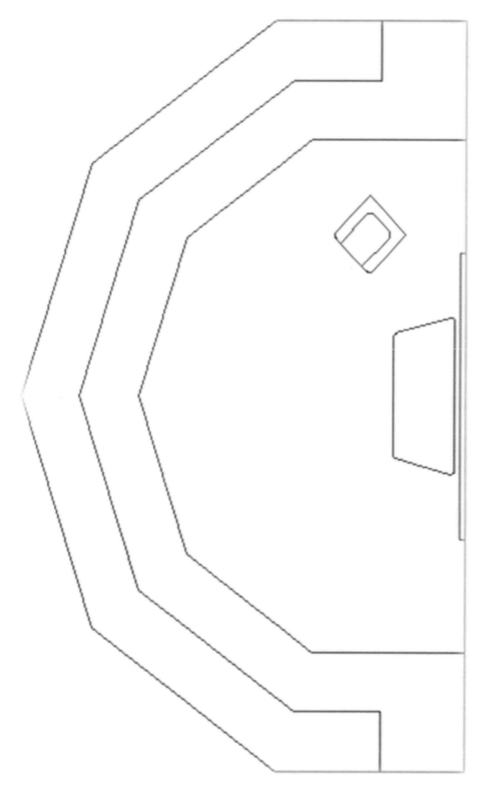

From *School Library Spaces: Just the Basics* by Patricia A. Messner and
Brenda S. Copeland. Santa Barbara, CA: Libraries Unlimited. Copyright © 2011.

FURNISHINGS

Story corners can be furnished simply with a rocking chair for the adult and space on the carpet for students. Others have wild-colored beanbag and lounge chairs that serve as motivation for good behavior. These special chairs can be used on a rotating schedule, and the ones chosen for the privilege must mind their manners to be able to keep that seat for story time. All other students sit on the floor or on a carpet square. If students talk or misbehave, they lose the seat and it goes to the next student on the list. Most libraries have one or two special chairs for this purpose. Just mark the attendance chart with a "c" for chair or a star. When everyone has had a turn, then rotate again. Some libraries have enough small on-the-floor lounge chairs or cushions for the entire class—if there is room. Possible sources are DEMCO and Highsmith.

Carpet tiles are used in many libraries and work well to keep students in their assigned spaces. These squares can be acquired at most local carpet stores. Many businesses will donate these to schools or at most charge a dollar or two. There are two ways that carpet squares can be managed. One is for the first class of the day to pick up a square on the way to the story corner. Students place the square in the correct spot and use it for that class period. When the group returns to the classroom, the students leave the squares behind for the next class. The last class of the day returns the squares to the collection pile that is designated by the staff. Alternatively, the library staff can do the arrangement of the squares at the beginning of the day and have the last class of the day collect and put away.

Another special way to dress up the library story corner is with an area rug. Companies like DEMCO have a variety of area reading rugs that can be placed directly on the floor or over carpet in the story area. They are colorful and add excitement to any space. Many have a theme that highlights a book character. DEMCO also carries a wide variety of chairs, including ottomans and beanbag chairs. See the resource section for address and contact information.

Bulletin and dry eraser boards are useful in the story corner if space is available. Bulletin boards decorated with the theme for the week or month spark students' interest in the story or activity. Dry eraser boards are helpful when engaging students in writing activities. Dry eraser boards are also magnetic and can be used for storytelling, with story items such as pictures, signs, or characters from the book. An easel with a dry eraser board attached can be used if there is no wall space for the mounting of boards. Also, a tablet of chart paper attached to the easel will serve as a writing surface.

SUPPLIES

Supplies are needed to help the library story corner program run smoothly. First of all, storage for writing supplies, such as a table with a plastic divided tub (purchased from Wal-Mart) or an everything cart sold by The Library Store, is a good idea. Writing supplies for staff and students can be stored in the tub or cart and might include pencils, pens, paper, clip boards, dry eraser markers, read-aloud books, and attendance sheets. To respect student privacy, do not leave attendance sheets out and available for others to see. The writing supplies can be used by staff for taking attendance, keeping track of overdue books not usually in a computerized program, and writing on the dry eraser board. Students will use the supplies for writing activities directed by the staff, such as recording facts from a nonfiction read-aloud. Puppets will need a good home in the story corner, such as a puppet tree or holder found at the John R. Green Company and other suppliers. If space is limited, the everything cart can be used for all the supplies, including the puppets. Also, an easel with storage underneath will work for supplies. When funds are not available to purchase puppets, high school students can be called upon to make puppets for stories. Industrial Arts students can build puppet trees or holders and also puppet theaters. Secondary students are always searching for service projects, so tap into these resources. Displaying puppets and supplies

Story corner supplies in a plastic caddy.

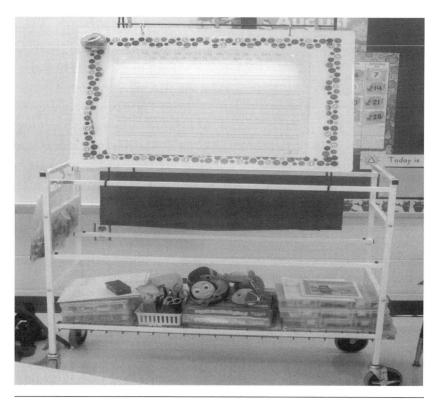

Easel with storage for supplies.

all the time might not be a good idea if the library is used by other staff and community members after school hours, so supplies and puppets should be mobile and easily locked up at night or displayed only when utilizing them for a read-aloud. Don't forget to replenish the supplies. Set aside a time to have students sharpen pencils, check the paper supply, and tidy up the supplies. See the resources section for information on purchasing supply containers, puppets, and puppet trees.

EQUIPMENT

How much equipment you can acquire for the story corner may be determined by the amount of money available, and you may need to purchase it over a few years due to budget restraints. The story corner does not need a lot of money to run effectively. However, technology does make the job a lot easier. Start off small, and work toward the higher priced items. Check several catalogs, and talk to the technology staff. Sometimes they are the ones that order for the district. Here are several items that work out best in the story corner.

A *microphone* for the staff member reading or talking to students in the story corner is an excellent idea. Students are able to sit and listen to the adult without the distractions of furnaces, air conditioners, and just general noise of other patrons coming and going.

Televisions, DVD and VHS players are useful in the story corner. Viewing books that have been made into DVDs or videos always sparks interest in the book. Another use for televisions and players is for showing a preview for a book fair. They can also be used as rewards for class behavior or for bringing back books and for special seasonal parties. Each school's policies for using DVDs, videos, and movies are different, so explore usage with building administrators.

Podcasting is sharing audio content over the Internet that can be downloaded. You don't need to have an iPod, just a computer with audio output. Scholastic has a top 10 best podcasting sites, which offer audio books, poems of the day, and book talks. See the resource section for Scholastic's website. Students can make their own podcasts and share them with others. Students can read to younger students, do reviews on books, and host podcast pals. Kid-Cast is a website that allows students to make their own podcasts. Check with your school's technology office about the downloading and audio capability of equipment.

Audio recordings of books can be used during story corner time. Invest in a stereo system with speakers and the ability to play audiocassettes and CDs. New buildings might have a sound system installed in the ceiling, but, if this is not available, purchase a cart for the stereo and speakers from DEMCO. Having the stereo on a cart can make it more mobile and a special treat for students. Most library store companies make audio recordings of books, complete with books.

The *overhead projector* has long been used in many libraries effectively. It projects overhead transparencies onto a screen or blank wall.

Overheads usually can be made at the workstation where the building copier is located. The black-and-white copy is fed into the machine, and the copier transfers the info onto the transparency. Special markers to use on the overheads can be purchased at any local office supply store; an example is the Expo Vis-à-vis Wet-Wipe Markers found at Demco.com. These markers make it possible to erase any items circled or blanks filled in. The transparency then can be used with numerous classes.

LCD projectors are hooked into the computer and projects onto the screen what appears on the computer monitor. News clips about books and authors can be pulled from the Internet and shared with students. Also, PowerPoint presentations about authors can be used with an LCD projector.

Smart boards are used with a dry eraser board, and the information accessed comes through the computer or laptop. The screen can be used with just a gentle touch. You can write with a pen and erase with your hand. This technology enables the staff person to move things around with the touch of just the fingers. Also, the library staff will be able to search the Internet, pull up charts, and play video clips for the story time.

Document cameras hook into an LCD projector or television and make it possible to project pages from a book onto the screen. This way, the class can read along with the staff. Some schools have televisions mounted on a wall in each classroom, while others have them on carts that are used by multiple classrooms. It works best if as much as possible of the equipment used in the story corner is on a movable cart. That way, when you do not need equipment or if there are space or other issues that develop in a busy day, you can move the cart to a back room or corner. This equipment cart may need to be used with an older class in another location. Portability makes it easy to access the equipment at any time and any place.

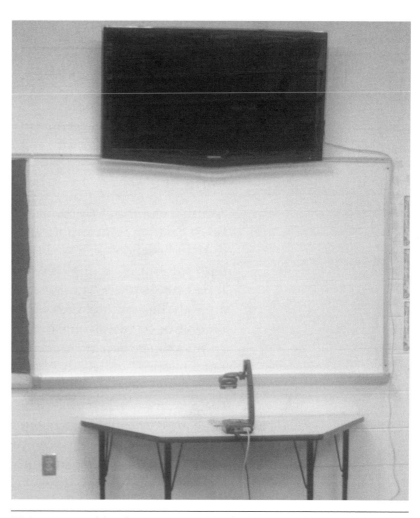

TV mounted in the story pit and a document camera attached.

DECORATING

LCD projector, laptop, and VCR on a cart.

Since the story corner is a gathering place for younger students to enjoy a story, decorating is a must. Some library staffs will want to decorate monthly and follow the holiday seasons and school events. This will take time and energy away from other library tasks, and storing of decorations can be an issue if space is limited. Other library staffs will choose to decorate the story corner with a yearly theme. Decorations are found at yard sales and thrift stores, and even friends and family are willing to be on the lookout for items. Items that might be needed are stuffed animals, pictures, toys, and costumes. The Library Store and DEMCO have decorations that can be purchased. Stenciling or painting a mural is a permanent way of decorating, and the art teacher is a resource if the library staff is uncomfortable about using paint. Decorating is well worth the effort because students will notice all the extras. Here are a few ideas.

Farm Theme

A farm theme is an easy theme to follow, since there are so many picture books relating to this topic. It can be used year round or at any time during the school year. A refrigerator box makes a good barn (see the barn pattern). Most appliance stores will supply one if they know it is for a school project. The art teacher has tempera paint and brushes, so tap into this resource. Create a space for the barn depending on the library layout, and use some stuffed farm animals for extra props. Stuffed animals can be purchased at yard sales and thrift stores. Also, raid your kids' toy chest, and ask for handouts from other school staff members. Mark items with pieces of masking tape with the donor's name if the person wishes to have them returned. Collect a large amount of bandana-type scarves. These can be placed in a basket, and, as students enter, they can put on their farm outfit. Fabric stores have collections of this type of fabric, so try cutting bandanas for this project. These can be used periodically for younger classes. Pick special stories or days to use this. If they are used too many times, the kids will lose their excitement and joy. Pull farm stories to put up a book display if there is room. Sometime during your story times, dress like a farmer, and greet the students as they enter. Jeans and a flannel shirt will work out fine.

STORY CORNER

Barn Pattern

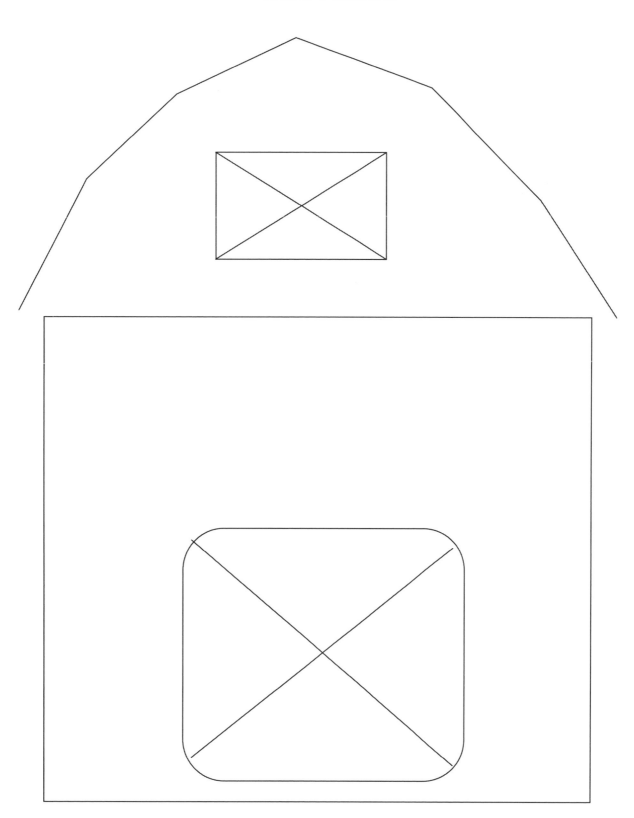

Pumpkin Patch Theme

Around the fall of the year is a wonderful time to turn the story pit into a pumpkin patch. Collect pumpkins and fall items like gourds and plastic fall leaves. Make a sign that states, "Welcome to the Pumpkin Patch." Use a bale of hay, and be daring. It can create a messy floor, and that might be a factor to explore. Make a scarecrow using old clothes. Stuffing can be plastic trash bags from the grocery store. Have a big scarecrow sitting on the hay, and have a Name Your Scarecrow contest for the month of October. The staff of course will dress as scarecrows. Tie into the school parties for the fall. Most schools are trying to steer away from the Halloween theme. Scarecrow Day is a better way to go. Check *The Mailbox* magazines for fall patterns for crows and pumpkins.

Garden Theme

Visit the local Home Depot or garden center, and scout out a piece of trellis or fencing that can be placed in the story pit, or make one from a refrigerator box (see the pattern for a garden fence). Collect gardening tools and gloves in a basket. Flowers made from tissue paper and green leaves cut from construction paper work well on the walls. Plastic or silk flowers and greens from your home closet will work for other decorations. Again, the local thrift stores and garage sales can be places to look for supplies. Birdhouses sitting around help with this theme. An Adirondack deck chair works well as a place for the story reader to sit.

STORY CORNER

Garden Fence Pattern

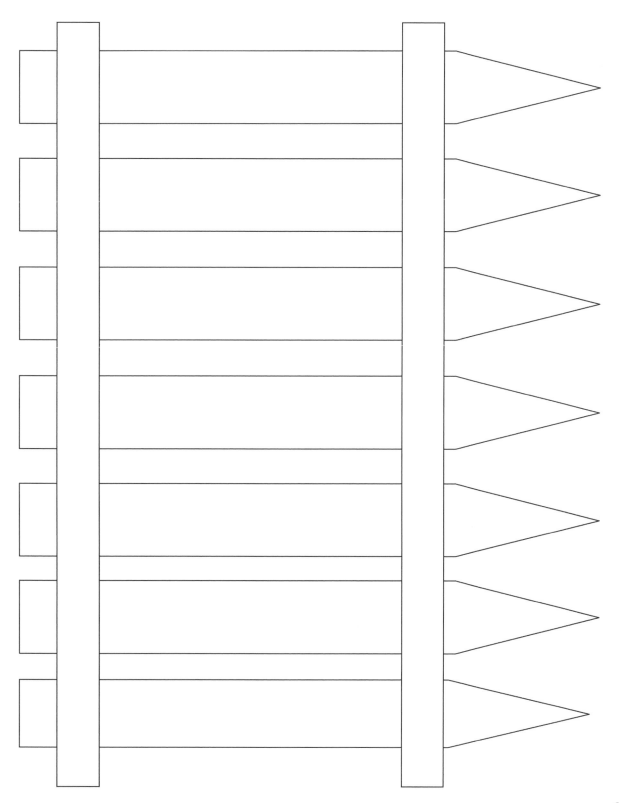

Rainforest trees.

Rainforest or Jungle

A jungle or rainforest theme is easily created by visiting the carpet store and requesting the tubes that carpet is rolled on. Cut tubes in different lengths and paint them with brown paint. Anchor trees with blocks of wood and a two-by-four attached and extended up the tube. Cut a leaf pattern out of green tissue paper and weave a wire through the center of the leaf, leaving extra wire to attach to the trunk. Vines can be made out of crepe paper. Add live plants for short foliage. Stuffed animals such as parrots, lizards, and monkeys can be collected from the local thrift store to complete the scene. See the photo for a sample.

Ship-Columbus Day

Another idea for the refrigerator box is to make the Santa Maria. See the accompanying picture for an example. Brown poster paint is used, along with jumbo black markers for adding details. Sailor hats and navy shirts make a simple costume for the library staff. Sails can be made out of bulletin board paper. The entrance to the story corner is the gang plank. Use rope to complete the effect.

Santa Maria ship as a story corner.

White House/President's Day

Cut the White House from a refrigerator box. See the sample picture for ideas. Poster paint from the art room works well for the exterior. Jumbo permanent markers will add the details for the windows and doors. Dress as George and Martha Washington or any other presidential couple. George's coat is a modified grey wool coat from the thrift store. White is used for the coat trim, and gold buttons from a sewing shop add detail.

George and Martha Washington costumes in front of the White House.

RESOURCES

COMPANIES

DEMCO
P.O. Box 7488
Madison, WI 53707-7488
www.demco.com

John R. Green Company
www.johnrgreenco.com

Highsmith
P.O. Box 5210
Janesville, WI 53547-5210
www.highsmith.com

LakeShore
2695 E. Dominguez Street
Carson, CA 90895
www.lakeshorelearning.com

The Library Store, Inc.
P.O. Box 0964

112 E. South Street
Tremont, Illinois 61568-0964
www.thelibrarystore.com

ABC School Supply
P.O. Box 369
Landisville, PA 17538
www.abcschoolsupply.com

BOOKS

Burkholder, Kelly. *Puppets.* Vero Beach, FL: Rourke Press, 2001.

Carreiro, Carolyn. *Make Your Own Puppets and Puppet Theaters.* Nashville, TN: Williamson Books, 2005.

Sadler, Wendy. *Puppets.* Chicago, IL: Heinemann Library, 2005.

WEBSITES

http://www2.scholastic.com/browse/article.jsp?id=11531
www.kid-cast.com

CHAPTER 3

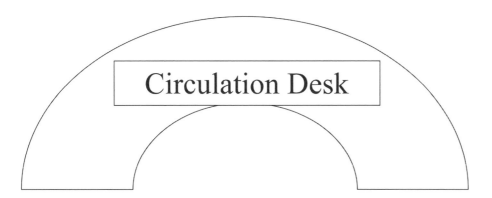

Circulation Desk

LOCATION

The circulation desk is the hub of any library. It is at this work station that the library staff checks materials in and out for the entire school. Teachers and students alike meet the library staff here. Whether the library uses an automated checkout system or the card-in-pocket version, the staff may need to keep a few things in mind as you set up this all important station in the library. The first and most important item to consider is whether the entire library can be easily seen from the spot chosen for the desk. Multitasking is a big part of the library day. For example, the library staff will have to check books in and out and keep an eye on the other patrons at the same time. Some libraries have self-checkout, but someone at the desk still has to monitor the process. Can the staff view all of the book sections and student computer stations from the checkout point? Also keep in mind the location of the main entrance. Anyone entering the library will need to be addressed and helped. Watch for blind spots, and angle the desk to cover these areas when possible. Some libraries have inside support columns that the desk attendant will have to see around.

Second, the checkout desk needs to have access to any Internet cables and phone jacks. In some libraries, this is the deciding factor for location. If cables can be run along the floor of a cabinet space, then the tech staff can drill a hole to feed the cords up through the counter to the computer space. Use plastic ties or clips to keep the cords out of the way of traffic and the movement of desk chairs.

Last, the circulation desk needs to be placed so that it does not interfere with traffic flow. Students need to know that there are places in the library that they need to be invited into or escorted to by an adult. If the desk is on a corner, then all space behind it might be consider a library-staff-only section. The layouts and photos in this chapter will suggest some options. It is best to plan your space out on paper before starting to move furniture. Once cables have been moved or rerouted, it is hard to have them changed.

CIRCULATION DESK

Layout #1

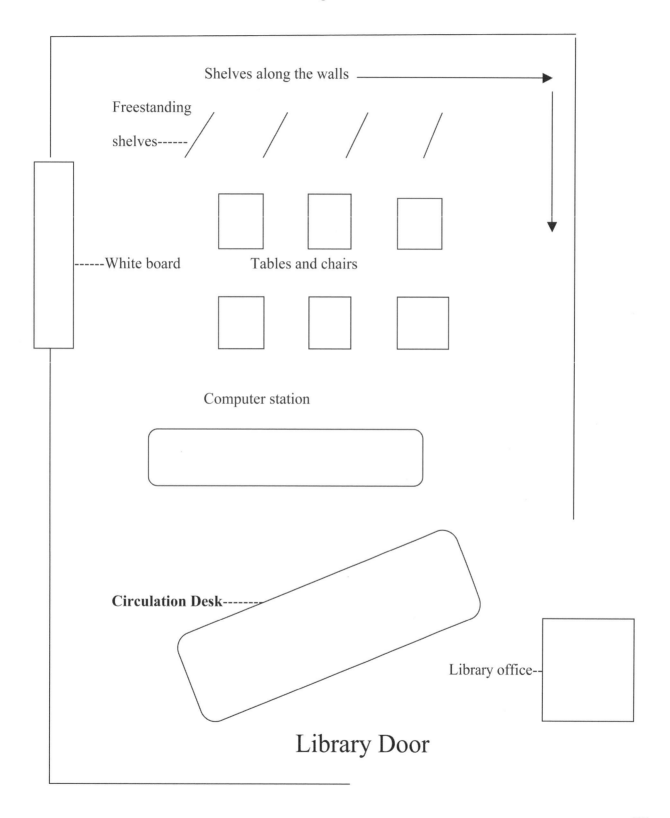

Shelves along the walls

Freestanding

shelves------

------White board

Tables and chairs

Computer station

Circulation Desk-------

Library office--

Library Door

From *School Library Spaces: Just the Basics* by Patricia A. Messner and Brenda S. Copeland. Santa Barbara, CA: Libraries Unlimited. Copyright © 2011.

CIRCULATION DESK

Layout #2

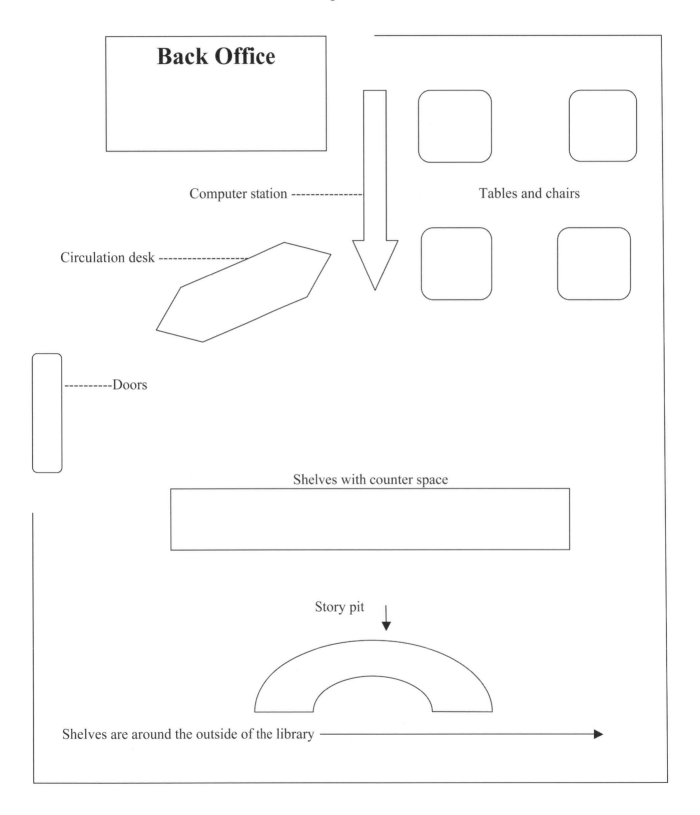

Back Office

Computer station --------------

Tables and chairs

Circulation desk -------------------

----------Doors

Shelves with counter space

Story pit

Shelves are around the outside of the library ————————————————→

CIRCULATION DESK

Layout #3

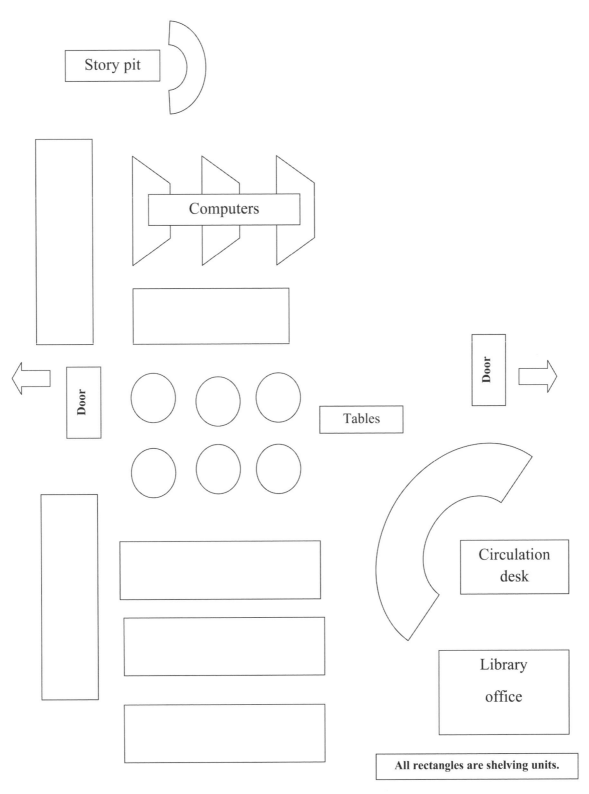

Story pit

Computers

Door

Door

Tables

Circulation desk

Library office

All rectangles are shelving units.

From *School Library Spaces: Just the Basics* by Patricia A. Messner and
Brenda S. Copeland. Santa Barbara, CA: Libraries Unlimited. Copyright © 2011.

CIRCULATION DESK
Layout #4

Circulation desk

Door

Computers

Story pit

Circulation desk.

SUPPLIES AND FURNISHINGS

Supplies are needed for the operation of the circulation desk. Basic supplies like pens, pencils, sticky notes, and paper are useful for writing down telephone messages, student and staff requests, and to-do lists. Pencils holders and letter trays are handy and can be stored on the circulation desk if space is not a problem. Also, a stapler and scotch tape and book repair tape in dispensers are helpful if included on the desk. See the accompanying photo of the top of a circulation desk. A couple of file drawers are useful for storing things like a receipt book, postage stamps, and other supplies that are not needed all the time. A telephone is necessary for resolving computer problems and the day-to-day issues that come up during the school day, such as communicating with parents and other patrons. A chair or stool will allow the staff to sit while taking care of

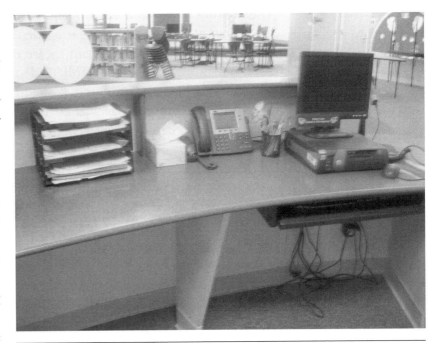

Circulation desk with supplies.

patrons. A computer and printer sit on the circulation desk if the library is automated.

SETUP OF CIRCULATION PROCEDURE

Most school libraries either have an automated checkout system or the old card-in-pocket method. At schools that are not automated, the library staff will need to use cards with a pocket for each library book. (See the diagram for a typical setup.) The pocket can be placed either in the front of the book or in the back. It is best to do one or the other consistently so that staff and students do not have to hunt for the card. Pockets and cards can be purchased from The Library Store or Gaylord or other supply vendors. Book pockets come with self-adhesive backs, so you just pull the tabs and stick the pocket on the inside of the library book. Stamp the front of the card with your school name. The book title, author, and call number will need to be typed on the cards. These cards have a space for the patron's name and room or class code or number. After students sign their name and code or number, the staff stamps the return date and collects all cards from this classroom, placing them in a drawer or some sort of sorting file (this is something else that is often on the circulation desk) for the next library visit. The drawer or file should contain dividers labeled for each classroom. With an automated system, each patron has a barcode. The computer recognizes patrons by their assigned barcode. Each book is labeled on the front cover with its own barcode. The patron barcodes can be organized either with an individual library card or with a list of barcodes for each class. Patrons with individual cards should have names and barcodes for each card. When the class enters to choose new library books, the cards for that class can be spread out on the table so that students can locate their name after making their book selection. The cards are collected after each visit and placed in a drawer under the teacher's name. If the library staff uses the list method, the patron name and barcode are on a class list. The list is placed in a notebook and kept on the circulation desk for easy access. The collection of lists is in order according to the scheduling of classes. Patron cards and then the book barcodes are scanned. The computer system does all of the work in keeping track of what goes out each day. See the resource page for companies that automate for libraries.

CIRCULATION DESK

Card Pocket

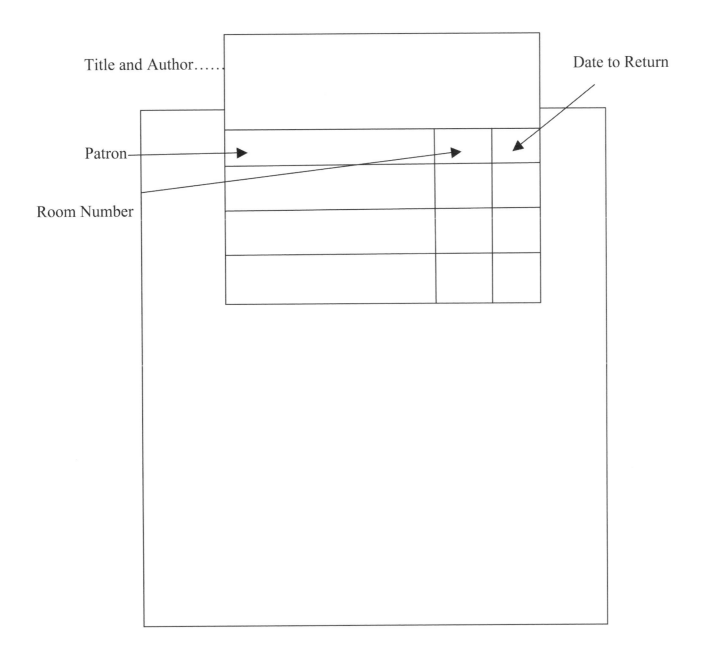

Title and Author......

Date to Return

Patron

Room Number

RESOURCES

AUTOMATION COMPANIES

Alexandria
www.goalexandria.com

Follett Software Company
www.follettsoftware.com

Keystone Library Automation System
www.klas.com

Mandarin Library Automation, Inc.
www.malasolutions.com

BOOK POCKET COMPANIES

Gaylord Bros.
P.O. Box 4901
Syracuse, NY 13221-4901
www.gaylord.com

The Library Store, Inc.
P.O. Box 0964
112 E. South Street
Tremont, IL 61568-0964
www.thelibrarystore.com

CHAPTER 4

Magazines and professional journals are resources that can be included in the library and are enjoyed by young and old patrons alike. Some librarians with small budgets might opt to use funds for books instead of purchasing different kinds of periodicals. They choose to limit the variety of periodicals and spend the biggest portion of their budget on books. Magazines do have a limited shelf life, so that is something to consider when making choices. Professional journals might be exempt from this rule. Libraries need to take professional journals for themselves and the other faculty. Periodicals (magazines, newspapers, journals) can be used in many different ways, and several questions can be asked when looking at this area of the library. First, will patrons just read these in the library, or will they be checked out? Both a display and a browsing area are needed if patrons are using materials in the library. Browsing shelves can be freestanding units, both spinning and stationary, or units that are connected to another

Display and browsing area for magazines with freestanding shelves.

Labels with names of magazines.

shelving unit or the wall. The display racks hold an assortment of magazines or other materials and can have a few pockets or several. Shelves can be made out of wood or metal. Display the newest issues, along with the past two months of each title. Arrange the magazines in alphabetical order on the browsing shelves. Attaching the name of the magazines to the front of the shelves will help keep order. Patrons can see the name of the magazine and replace it in the correct spot. Stressing this helps the library staff keep things in order. Plastic covers preserve the life of the magazine or journal and can be ordered from any library store supply company. There are several different kinds of covers. The inexpensive ones fall apart, so it is best to invest in more expensive covers. When the magazine issues are older and ready to be moved to storage, the plastic covers are then placed on the newest issues. The browsing and reading areas should be in an open space so that staff can supervise patrons. Don't hide the browsing area behind regular book shelves. The photos in this chapter will give you an idea of the kinds of arrangements available.

Will patrons check magazines out? If magazines are to be checked out by patrons, both the new issue and older issues should be displayed for easy access. Slanted shelves work well for the new copies, but older copies may need to be in cardboard or plastic bins and require standard shelves. Also, some slanted magazine shelves have storage under the shelves for older issues. The slanted shelves lift up. More walking-around space is needed for patrons to take time to browse while choosing magazines to take home.

Finally, will patrons use magazines for research? Some magazines might be requested for a research topic, and the library staff may need to pull a group of magazines for a classroom assignment. For example, if a fourth-grade class is working on animal reports, the librarian could pull old issues of *Zoobook* magazine to help with this project. If they are stored in the back office and are labeled, they can easily be made available for a special class time. Ideally, a separate library classroom with the outside walls lined with magazine shelves and the middle of the room filled with tables and chairs allows a classroom of students to do research and use the magazines. Also, having a few computers allows students to do online searching to find magazine citations. There might also be shelving for the *Reader's Guide to Periodical Literature*. If a student has located an article online and wishes

Magazines with covers on shelves.

to have it made available, the librarian can pull it from the back storage shelves. Newspapers are useful to find current events, and both staff and students will benefit from any subscriptions. Some communities offer free subscription to the local paper to area schools. Display is usually on shelves, and the newspapers are stacked on top of each other. The accompanying photo illustrates this. Older issues of newspapers are hard to store, so most school libraries keep them for only a week or two. Many newspapers are also found online, so back issues can be accessed. The art department will usually take old newspapers for projects, or most schools have a recycling program for paper.

Many libraries purchase teacher magazines and books for the staff. A special spot with a comfortable seating area in a backroom or office works well for this. Some librarians and staff keep special treats, such as candy, for the staff as a way of providing them a comfortable, inviting place to look at new materials and to interest them in checking them out. Magazines and new books that need to be drawn to the staff's attention can be displayed together. Create a warm, cheery spot that will draw staff into the library by providing comfortable chairs, reading lamps, a coffee pot, and so on. A table works for staff

Display of magazines with shelves attached to another shelving unit.

magazines if there is not room for shelves and a reading area. The photo shows a suggested arrangement. The newest copies can be on display, and older copies can be in a storage area that staff can access if necessary. Some libraries route popular magazines to the staff by placing them into staff mailboxes with a checkoff box so that staff will look at them and then pass them on to the next interested teacher. For example, you can route *The Kindergarten Mailbox* to all kindergarten teachers. The last teacher on the list will bring it back to the library.

Older issues of magazines can be stored in a back room or on shelves out of the main traffic areas. Cardboard and plastic file boxes are made for this purpose. Label the boxes with the name of the magazine and the year, and arrange the issues from oldest to newest. At the end of the year, most libraries remove the oldest periodicals from the collection, keeping four or five years of back issues.

Classroom teachers, resource classrooms, and art departments enjoy using old copies for special projects, so do not be afraid to offer these to staff.

Slanted metal shelves with lift-up storage.

Storage of newspapers.

Display of professional materials.

Storage of old magazines.

RESOURCES

DEMCO
P.O. Box 7488
Madison, WI 53707-7488
www.demco.com

Gaylord Bros.
P.O. Box 4901
Syracuse, NY 13221-4901
www.gaylord.com

The Library Store, Inc.
P.O. Box 0964
112 E. South Street
Tremont, IL 61568-0964
www.thelibrarystore.com

CHAPTER 5

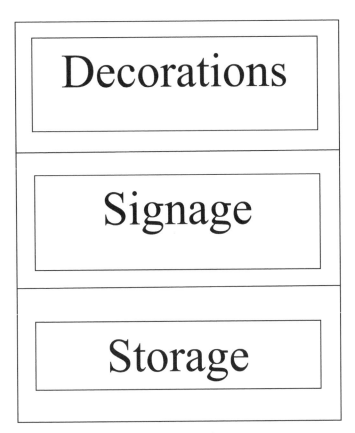

DECORATIONS

Decorations make the library student-friendly, and students enjoy the extra time the staff spends on decorating the library. Purchase or make decorations to enhance the atmosphere of the library. Most library supply companies provide premade decorations. See the resource page for examples. Die cutters, computers, printers, and copy machines are helpful when making decorations. Die cutters can be used for letters, objects such as apples, pumpkins, script letters and numbers, and many other options. Pictures or objects can be printed from the Internet using a computer and a printer. Decorations can be found in teacher magazines and can be copied, colored, and laminated. Make sure to consider copyright restrictions. Decorating the library can be by the month or season, or you can buy a special theme that can be added to throughout the year. Seasonal decorations can be purchased when they are marked down at the end of the season sales and tucked away for the next school year.

STORAGE OF DECORATIONS AND BULLETIN BOARDS

Decorations can be stored in cardboard or plastic boxes. Plastic boxes last longer, and the contents are visible without even opening the box. Attach content labels to the end or side of the boxes, and stack them on shelves. The graphics illustrated in this chapter may give you ideas for labels. A closet or a back room with several shelving units works well for storage. Keep boxes in the order they are used throughout the school year. Before putting them away each time, toss out old or tired items. Sometimes you need to have letters or pictures replaced. Keeping up with them as you use them makes the next year run more smoothly. New items can be added as you find them if you have an orderly arrangement of boxes. Bulletin boards can be stored in extra-large plastic bags and then placed inside boxes or in a drawer. Some libraries have a standing flat-file drawer that makes storing posters and bulletin boards easier. Theses flat-file units have drawers that are not really deep but are wide enough to accommodate larger size materials such as posters and flat art prints. Label the drawers as needed.

SIGNAGE IDEAS

Library Word Wall

Many classroom teachers post words that their grade levels need to learn during the school year. They start with a few and add words as they are introduced. In the library, the staff can do the same thing for words associated with libraries. The visual connection to words that are covered in the library during the year can be a real benefit to students. Find a wall or space that can be decorated in an eye-catching manner. Type words out on the computer and paste them onto construction paper. Laminate the words so that they can be used each year. As the words are covered or highlighted in the lessons, add them to your wall. Another option is to change the words after the first semester. Use a different color scheme for the second-semester words so that students pick up on the change. Some school supply stores even sell plastic pocket foldouts that can be used for word wall displays. Space may be an issue, and in some of these cases a blank wall above shelving units works best. That leaves your main bulletin board free for seasonal or reading themes. See diagram for layout ideas.

Website Wall

A website wall can be displayed just like a word wall. Use banner-making software programs like Publisher or Print Shop to make the letters in the website address. The website address will print out on multiple pieces of paper, so cut the extra paper off and tape the words together to form a long banner; then laminate it and hang up.

Restroom and Hall Passes

Restroom and hall passes can be printed out on a color printer, laminated, and attached to a necklace made of yarn or string. Hang passes from plastic hooks purchased at Wal-Mart. Hooks can be placed near the door.

Behavioral Expectations

Library behavioral expectations can be posted in the room. Use a die cut or print from a computer, paste it on poster board, laminate, and hang it up.

Labels for Things in the Library

Purchase or make signage for things in the library. If a banner program is available, make banners to label each section of the library, along with the story pit, magazines, and so on. A color printer makes the banners eye-catching. Laminate both kinds for longer use.

Examples of the signage ideas discussed here are illustrated in the photos and graphics in this chapter.

Library Word Wall

Spine

Dewey

Biography

Title

Author

Fiction

Nonfiction

DECORATIONS, SIGNAGE, AND STORAGE

Website Wall Graphic

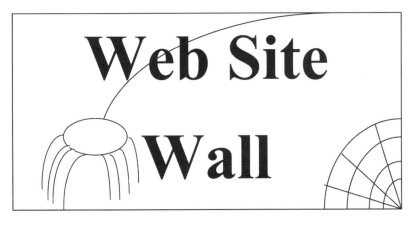 

www.funschool.com

www.primarygames.com

www.starfall.com

www.aplusmath.com

www.funbrain.com

www.pbskids.org/arthur

www.kidsplanet.org

www.spellingcity.com

Fall

Winter

Spring

Summer

Thanksgiving

St. Patrick's Day

Christmas

Valentine's Day

September

October

November

December

January

February

March

DECORATIONS, SIGNAGE, AND STORAGE

Sign Graphic

April

May

June

DECORATIONS, SIGNAGE, AND STORAGE

Restroom and Hall Pass Graphics

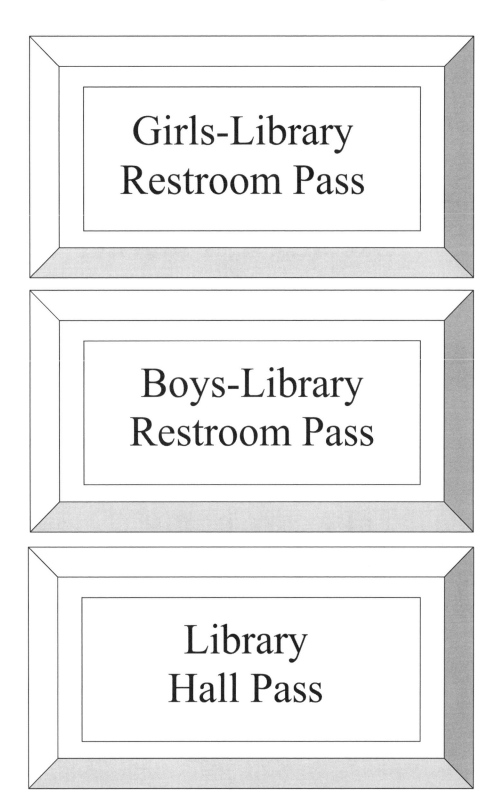

Girls-Library
Restroom Pass

Boys-Library
Restroom Pass

Library
Hall Pass

DECORATIONS, SIGNAGE, AND STORAGE

Behavior Guidelines Graphic

> ## In the Library I will.......
>
> ### Use an inside voice.
>
> ### Use my shelf marker correctly.
>
> ### Check out my books at the desk.
>
> ### Put supplies away. Take care of my book.
>
> ### Push my chair in.

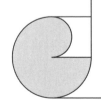

Fiction

Easy

Biography

Nonfiction

Labels for Things in the Library

Computers

Story Corner

Magazines

Circulation Desk

RESOURCES

Library Skills, Inc.
P.O. Box 469
West End, NC 27376-0469
www.libraryskills.com

Ellison
25862 Commercentre Drive
Lake Forest, CA 92630-8804
www.ellisoneducation.com

Vernon Library Supplies, Inc.
2851 Cole Court
Norcross, GA 30071
www.vernonlibrarysupplies.com

CHAPTER 6

Bulletin boards are a common sight in most elementary schools. They appear on blank walls in various lengths and cause many anxious moments throughout the year as staff agonizes over their creation. Even though the task of keeping them changed and current is daunting, bulletin boards can be a great teaching resource in the library media center. The library staff can highlight a wide range of curricular subjects as well as seasonal themes, author visits, and fun reading. Patrons, parents, and staff can be reminded daily that the library is a special place, and learning does take place there. So it is important to use this avenue not only as a learning tool but also as an advertisement for the library program. Do not resort to putting up the same tired pictures each year. Having several standbys or old favorites that can be put up at a moment's notice is always a good idea, but have new ideas that can be worked on as needed for lessons and schoolwide activities. Looking in catalogs and magazines is a good way to get an idea that can be stretched into a bulletin board. Also, keep an assortment of up-to-date book jackets because incorporating these into a display always draws in that reluctant reader. Having titles front and center gives students a focus when they come to look up books to read. They will beg to be the next one to read that book. In this chapter we offer a few favorites that can be used and adapted for any space in the library.

CALENDAR IDEAS

December and January are great times to check out the new calendars for the coming year. Often, after the first of the year, prices are reduced and very affordable. Book characters, movie themes, famous places, and patriotic icons are found on calendars and will make great bulletin boards for the coming year. It is important to be careful about using copyrighted images from movies, characters (e.g., Disney characters), without permission. Cut the pictures apart, and laminate them. Use the die-cut machine to add related objects and words to complete the bulletin board. These bulletin boards can be saved for times during the year when a quick change is needed. They can also be turned into library-related subjects and curricular needs.

NEW BOOKS

Sometime at the beginning of the school year when the new book order arrives, take off dust jacket paper covers from several books. Collect an assortment of both easy and harder books. Use these to do a reading bulletin board. Cut out letters to make titles like "New on the Shelf," "Check These Out," or "Just Arrived at Our School." It is always amazing how many students will notice and want to read those books. Create a signup list so interested students can get the books before they go out into regular circulation.

INTERACTIVE BOARDS

An interactive bulletin board works well for any subject that you might be highlighting in the library. This type of board is set up so that the students are asked to do something. Sometimes this is writing a response and handing it in to the teacher. Other times the doing process is just answering the questions silently or completing the task (e.g., matching pictures to pockets).

Examples

1. **Presidents' Day Matchup.** Find pictures of presidents when they were younger, and put them up on the board. The students then match the picture of the president as a boy with the picture of him when he held office. This is a fun one for February, when we celebrate Presidents' Day. Make the board similar to the graphic page for the Dewey match. Pick a place that allows kids to work at the project; check your traffic flow when deciding where they should work.

2. **Do You Know Your Call Numbers?** Write or cut out letters to spell out "Fiction," "Easy," "Nonfiction," and "Biography,"

attach them to four sheets of 8½ × 11 construction paper, and staple them to the board. Staple around the bottom and sides of each piece of paper to form a pocket at the top. Copy examples of spine labels onto card stock and then cut out and laminate them. Attach a fifth 8½ × 11 piece of construction paper to the bottom of the bulletin board. Place the laminated spine labels in the fifth pocket. Dress up the rest of the board with seasonal pictures or book jackets. See the illustration to view how this looks.

3. **Put the Books in Shelf Order.** Cut letters for the title of the activity, and attach it to the board. Staple clear plastic sleeves to the board in one row. Using the call numbers from "Do You Know Your Call Numbers?," have students put the call numbers in shelf order by placing the call number in the plastic sleeve. Use only call numbers from one section of the library.

4. **Story Elements.** After reading a book to students, have them test their listening skills by placing the characters, setting, problem, and solution in the correct pocket.

5. **How Do You Find a Book?** Use the row of plastic sleeves, and have students sequence the process of finding a book in the library. Here is an example: Log onto the computer. Open the online catalog. Search for a title, author, or subject. Write down the title and call number. Find book on the shelf. Check out book at the desk.

STAR CLASSES

Reward classes with stars for good behavior or for returning all books. Every week that the students earn a star, place a star on the paper with the teacher's name on the star classes' bulletin board. If you don't have space for a bulletin board, stencil a star pattern on the wall to make a border and tape paper with teachers' names inside the pattern. Locate the star classes' bulletin board near the story corner if at all possible.

CHRISTMAS SUPER-SURPRISES

During the holiday season, plan to stress award-winning books by creating this easy bulletin board that will tie together the holidays and great books. Create a tree with packages at the bottom. Packages can be made by covering lids of small boxes with colorful wrapping paper. They can be stapled or tacked to the bulletin board. Make sure you decorate with bows and ribbons for added zip. See the graphic for the layout. Many times publishers advertise by giving libraries posters with award-winning books displayed on them. Follett is just one company that does this every year. Cut the pictures of the books apart, and attach the pictures to circles or bells cut from construction paper. The die-cut machine will give you some other choices. Decorate the pictures with glitter, and staple them to the tree. Newbery, Caldecott, and Coretta Scott King awards are just a few you can pick from. This is an easy way to get the students thinking of great titles.

PRIZE-WINNING PATRONS

Create a bulletin board or space in the library that can be divided into four sections for the four marking periods of the school year. See the graphic for an illustration. At the end of each marking period, post a list of classroom teachers and the students from that class who have brought back their library books each week. Students must have a perfect record in order to get on the list. The library staff may need to stress this at the beginning of school. When attendance is taken, mark whether the student brought back books along with the attendance tally. The goal is to have students' names listed for each marking period. The students who have their name on the list for the entire school year can receive a prize at the end of the year or plan a special party. Decorate your board with school colors and the team mascot. This promotes school spirit as well as responsibility. Students will love seeing whether they appear on the list. This will help with circulation and help keep the books coming back to the library.

VOTE FOR YOUR FAVORITE BOOK!

Select five new read-alouds to read to the classes prior to election day. Decorate a bulletin board with the theme "Vote for Your Favorite Book!" After reading all five books, ask students to color in a section above their favorite book. Talk about how parents and other adults vote on election day.

FRIEND TO BOOKS

In the early days of the school year, it is always necessary to talk to students about book care. Many librarians read books to classes and brainstorm ways to take care of the borrowed books before students check them out for the new school year. Create a bulletin board to highlight this by collecting various items that would be helpful or not helpful in preserving books, such as crayons, pencils, bookmarks, book bags, tissues, juice boxes, scissors, soap for clean hands, candy wrappers, pictures of dogs or cats, picture of a toddler, and gum wrappers. Staple or hot-glue them to the board. Attach letters for across the top that read "Friend or Not a Friend" or "Are You Careful?" This can be a teaching tool to remind kids that some things are harmful to our library books. Too many books come back all chewed up or ripped by a pet or younger sibling. If possible, have examples nearby of damaged books. These can be placed in a pocket in the corner of the board or on a counter. If the display is not near the bulletin board, then print up a sign explaining what happened. (e.g., This library book came back all chewed up. What can be done to keep books away from pets? What would good advice be to this friend?).

READ EVERY AWESOME DAY THIS SUMMER!

Promote summer reading with this bulletin board. Provide lists for students to take home and use at the public library. There are websites that offer lists for readers, and rewards can be given when students read books from the lists and return lists of books read signed by a parent.

Here are a couple of websites with ideas on summer reading lists:

http://childrensbooks.about.com/od/forparents/tp/summer_reading.htm
http://www.kidsreads.com/lists/classic-lists.asp
http://kids.nypl.org/reading/recommended.cfm

I JUST READ THE BEST BOOK!

Students can be critics by reading books and writing a short review. Take pictures of the students with the book and display the photos with the reviews. A dust jacket from the book will also spark students' interest. See the graphic for more details.

BIBLIOGRAPHY

The upper elementary classes throughout the school year will be doing lots of projects, PowerPoints, and reports. Teachers will ask for help with the process of teaching students how to write up a bibliography. This is a good way to stay ahead of the game. Putting the concepts in written form on the board helps to cement this important information. See the graphic for the layout. Stress the five components of a bibliography by printing them up on a computer or by cutting out the letters to form the words.
The five components are:

1. Title
2. Author
3. Publisher
4. Place of publication
5. Copyright date

BULLETIN BOARDS

Interactive Graphic

Dewey Match

398.2

513

811

636

910

463

743

Inside this pocket, put your book titles or categories. (Fairy tales, Drawing, Poetry, Pets, Math, Spanish, and Titanic) Type up words on cards and laminate. You can also use book jackets or pictures of the front of books.

Interactive Bulletin Board Idea Graphic

Do You Know Your Call Numbers?

Easy

Fiction

Nonfiction

Biography

Spine Labels

From *School Library Spaces: Just the Basics* by Patricia A. Messner and Brenda S. Copeland. Santa Barbara, CA: Libraries Unlimited. Copyright © 2011.

BULLETIN BOARDS

Cards for Do You Know Your Call Numbers?

E BRO	E BRI	E CAR	E WIL	E WEL	E ZOL
E GIB	E PAL	E SEU	E RYL	E BUN	E REY
F PAR	F BAB	F BLU	F BRO	F OSB	F WIL
F DIS	F DAD	F JON	F HAD	F MES	F COP
B LIN	B WAS	B KEL	B PAR	B KIN	B JOR
B GOR	B FLO	B WIL	B AAR	B POC	B BUS
398.2 GIB	796.33 LEA	912 KON	133.2 NOB	636.7 PAR	220.5 BIB
425 FRE	599.7 LEE	818 ROS	001.22 HIL	636.8 CAR	796.34 SOS

BULLETIN BOARDS

Star Classes

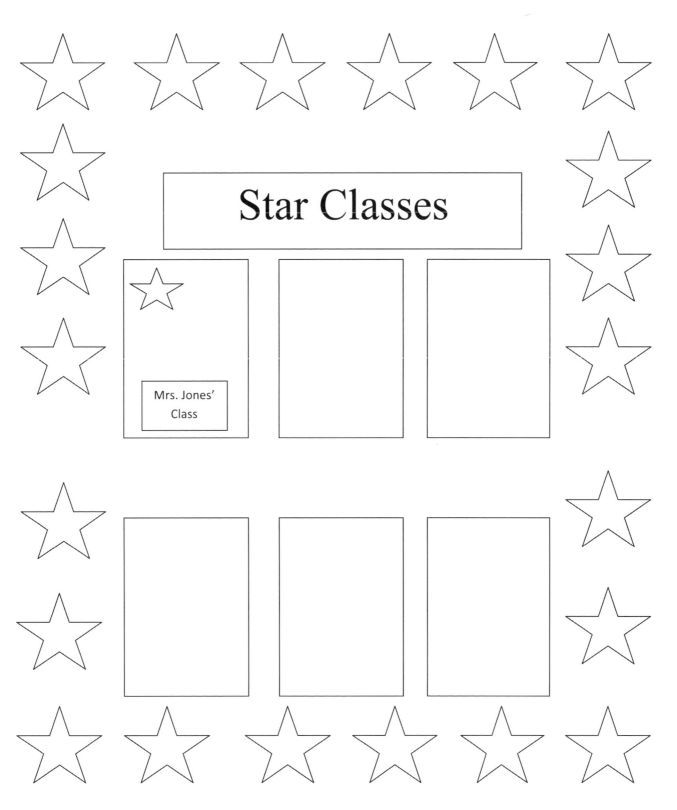

Star Classes

Mrs. Jones' Class

BULLETIN BOARDS

Caldecott Graphic

<u>Super Surprises</u>

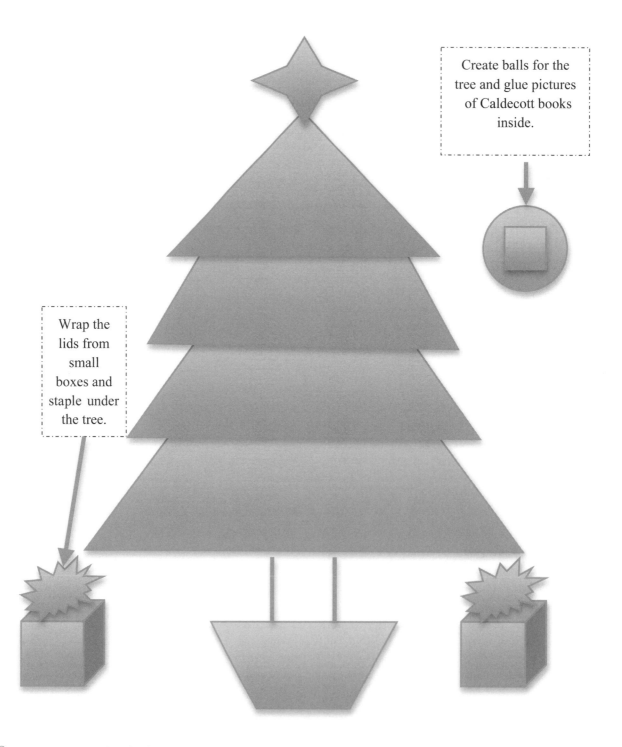

Create balls for the tree and glue pictures of Caldecott books inside.

Wrap the lids from small boxes and staple under the tree.

BULLETIN BOARDS

Prize-Winning Patrons Graphic

Prize Winning Patrons

First Marking Period

Second Marking Period

Third Marking Period

Fourth Marking Period

BULLETIN BOARDS

Vote for Your Favorite Book

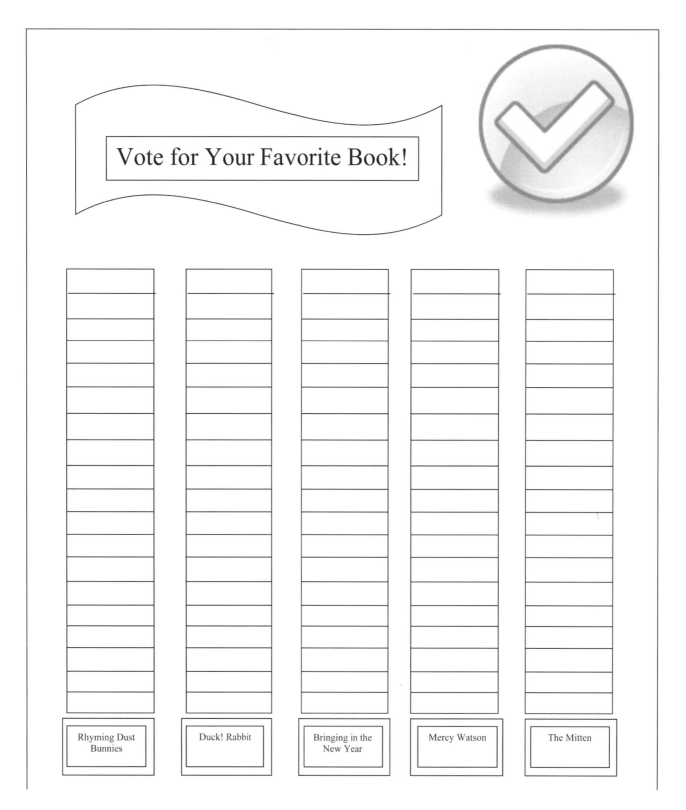

Vote for Your Favorite Book!

| Rhyming Dust Bunnies | Duck! Rabbit | Bringing in the New Year | Mercy Watson | The Mitten |

BULLETIN BOARDS

Read Every Awesome Day This Summer!

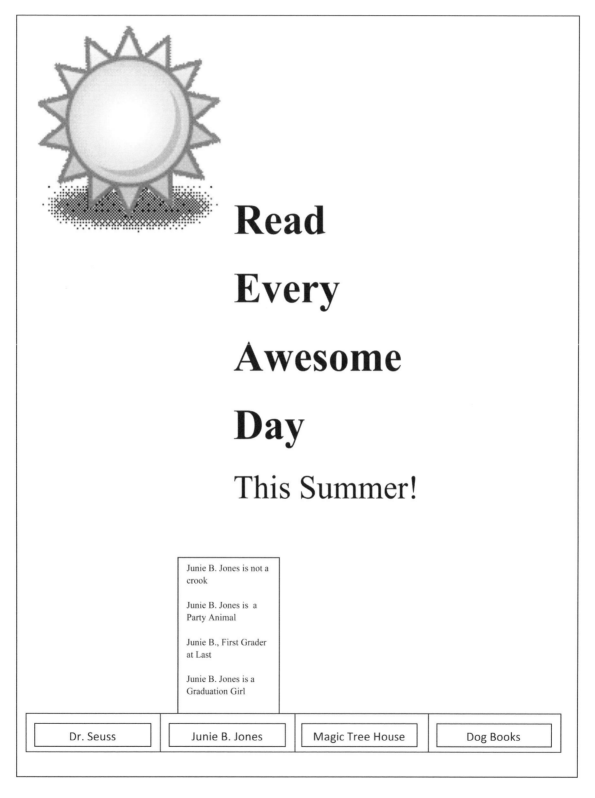

Read

Every

Awesome

Day

This Summer!

Junie B. Jones is not a crook

Junie B. Jones is a Party Animal

Junie B., First Grader at Last

Junie B. Jones is a Graduation Girl

| Dr. Seuss | Junie B. Jones | Magic Tree House | Dog Books |

BULLETIN BOARDS

I Just Read the Best Book!

I Just Read the Best Book!

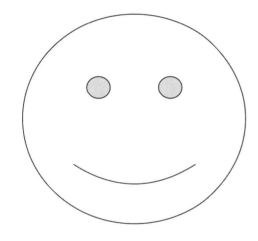

Title_____

Author_____

I liked this book
because_____

_____
_____
_____

BULLETIN BOARDS

Bibliography Graphic

Bibliography

When writing a bibliography, we need 5 components. Do you know where to find these?

Author

Title

Publisher

Copyright Date

Place of Publication

RESOURCES

http://childrensbooks.about.com/od/forparents/tp/summer_reading.htm
http://www.kidsreads.com/lists/classic-lists.asp
http://kids.nypl.org/reading/recommended.cfm

Evan-Moor Educational Publishing
18 Lower Ragsdale Drive
Monterey, CA 93940-5746
www.evan-moor.com

Teacher Created Materials, Inc.
6421 Industry Way
Westminster, CA 92683
www.teachercreated.com

Teacher's Friend Publications
A Scholastic Company
Riverside, CA
www2.scholastic.com/browse/teach.jsp

BOOKS

The Best of Mailbox Bulletin Boards, Book 2. Greensboro, NC: Education Center, 2004.

Cheyney, Jeanne S. *Big Book of Bulletin Boards for Every Month.* Tucson, AZ: Good Year Book, 2006.

Radcliffe, Loralyn. *Big and Easy Patterns.* Westminster, CA: Teacher Created Materials, Inc., 2004.

Sevaly, Karen. *Spring! Idea Book.* Riverside, CA: Teacher's Friend Publications, 2001.

CHAPTER 7

Furnishings

TABLES

Tables for the library come in round, square, or rectangular shapes. The two factors that need to be considered when choosing tables for any library are class size and room size. Square and round tables can be used for larger open library spaces. Rectangular tables work well if you have large classes and limited floor space. Square tables seat four patrons, round four to five patrons, and rectangular tables six to eight patrons. Map out your table space with masking tape and see what works best before making purchases. Most tables can be adjusted to different heights. If an area has only young patrons, the tables may need to be lower. Some libraries have separate classrooms for older classes, so the height issue is not a problem. These separate classrooms usually have tables and chairs for an average class of students. Sometimes these classrooms have only chairs. If this is the plan, then it might be wise to select chairs with a movable tablet arm.

Wheelchair Accessibility

The space from the top of the tables or counters to the floor needs to be between 28 to 34 inches high in order to accommodate wheelchairs. This is the regulation height for seating for adults (any patron over 13 years old). Visit ADA.gov and click on "ADA Design Standards" for guidelines regarding federal regulations.

CHAIRS

Chairs are available in various types and at various prices. If chairs need to be stacked so that the library space can be used for other events and school activities, keep this in mind. Some chairs also are heavy for elementary students to move around. Remember that some chairs will tip over if students tilt them back so make sure all four legs are on the floor. Chairs that look great may not be the ones that are the best for your library. If possible, try them out before making a purchase. Visiting other libraries is beneficial so visit, ask questions and take notes.

TABLES VERSUS CARRELS

Computer tables work well for a lab configuration. Some libraries have a large area for computers, and the staff will instruct the whole class on computers. An LCD projector and screen will be needed to complete the lab. The tables can be regular tables, but computer tables with holes for the cords are ideal. The holes allow the cords to be drawn through and attached to the tables underneath, making the tables neat and free from cords. If you are using regular tables without the holes, the cords can be bundled together with ties behind the computers. A lab in the library is not as pleasing to the eyes as study carrel work stations. When planning a new library, take into consideration whether to have a lab or study carrels. A separate room for the lab is a much better use of space.

Study carrels have several uses: study area for patrons and computer work stations. Carrels are useful if students are completing individual assignments or taking tests. They are large and take up precious space, so small areas might be crowded if you use carrels. Supervision of patrons is difficult because the staff will have limited visibility. Study carrels can be used as computer work stations. Purchase carrels that do not have high sides to deal with the visibility issue. Seating can consist of stools or chairs, or patrons can stand.

CASUAL READING AREA

A casual reading area makes the library homey and cozy. Select furniture that is easy to keep clean and that does not collect bugs. Donated items will work if money is an issue. Lamps and lighting devices are additive mood enhancements. Colorful rugs can highlight the area and are eye catching. End tables, bean bags, and stuffed animals are other options. Staff and students will enjoy this special area. Locate the area near magazines, newspapers, and/or the Easy section.

BOOK CARTS

Book carts can be helpful to any library. The two basic types are wood or steel, with either two or three shelves. The steel ones work well in the elementary setting because they come in different colors. This helps when students are ask to put their books on carts after they check them in. If possible, choose a different color for each category of books. For example, you can have a Nonfiction cart, a Fiction cart, and an Everybody/Easy cart. If the carts are labeled with signs, this will help the staff with the shelving process, because the books are then already sorted. It is also good practice for students learning the call numbers for each type of book. Other libraries prefer wooden carts that are all alike. Whatever your choice, keep in mind that it is a good idea to have an extra cart in the back office or work area. When you are processing the books, it can come in handy. The cart can be wheeled out of the way when it is not needed. When teachers request materials for a project or lesson, a cart can make it easier to transport them to another classroom.

LIBRARY OFFICE

Ideally, every library needs an office. When looking for office furnishings, keep in mind what is needed the most, and then add other items as space and budget permit. Check school policy before decorating the walls with stenciling or wallpaper. Some libraries have only a back corner for an office, while others have a rather large room adjacent to the main library. Three things come to mind that are necessary: file cabinets, desk, and desk chair. Teachers' desks come in three basic types: single pedestal to the right, single pedestal to the left, and the double pedestal. If possible, chose the double pedestal type because it gives more drawer space. The desk needs to be close to the telephone and computer outlets, so arrange the furniture accordingly. Another item to consider might be counter space for processing, or, if this is not available, a table will work. Some staff like to stand while doing jobs, while others would rather have a stool. If possible, pick a stool that is adjustable. Most find book shelves to be helpful. Many schools have workbooks and manuals that are kept on these shelves. Also, when new books arrive, they can be out of sight on a shelf until the processing work is done. If no separate office space is available, pick furniture that will keep the space off limits to patrons. Some companies have desk and credenzas that connect with panels to configure a space that will work.

STORAGE CABINETS

All libraries need storage cabinets, and space is the biggest factor when you are making choices. Cabinets work better if they can be placed in the library office or workroom. Lots of storage makes life easier for the staff. Cabinets come in fixed or mobile varieties. A typical arrangement is shown in the photograph. When shopping for cabinets, keep in mind that there are jumbo, combination, and office/wardrobe closets. Art and posters can be best stored in lateral flat files. These files can be easily stacked on top of each other if several drawers are needed. The drawers are designed for all flat materials and are a must-have item for school libraries. Mixed-media cabinets are ideal for storage of all multimedia materials. The drawers come with dividers for easy separation of materials and also have gliders so that the drawers can be extended to view items that are at the back. CD and DVD displays can make the collections more browser friendly. Adjustable dividers keep the cases organized and upright. An example is provided in the photograph. These displays come in mobile and fixed varieties and in a wide assortment of styles. When making choices, keep in mind that if general patrons are going to be signing out CDs and DVDs, the displays will need to be included in the layout of the main library. If these will be circulating only among staff, then they can be housed in the workroom or library office. Some displays take up lots of room but are very eye catching. A larger collection will need more shelves. Keep this in mind when making choices.

Poster storage and small storage room

Open metal shelves

Open wooden shelves and wall brackets

RESOURCES

www.ADA.gov

DEMCO
P.O. Box 7488
Madison, WI 53707-7488
www.demco.com

RESOURCES

COMPANIES

ABC School Supply
P.O. Box 369
Landisville, PA 17538
www.abcschoolsupply.com

Brodart Supplies and Furnishings
100 North Road, P.O. Box 300
McElhattan, PA 17748
www.shopbrodart.com

DEMCO
P.O. Box 7488
Madison, WI 53707-7488
www.demco.com

Ellison
25862 Commercentre Drive
Lake Forest, CA 92630-8804
www.ellisoneducation.com

Evan-Moor Educational Publishing
18 Lower Ragsdale Drive
Monterey, CA 93940-5746
www.evan-moor.com

Gaylord Bros.
P.O. Box 4901
Syracuse, NY 13221-4901
www.gaylord.com

John R. Green Company
www.johnrgreenco.com

Highsmith
PO Box 5210
Janesville, WI 53547-5210
www.highsmith.com

LakeShore
2695 E. Dominguez St.
Carson, CA 90895
www.lakeshorelearning.com

Library Skills, Inc.
P.O. Box 469
West End, NC 27376-0469
www.libraryskills.com

The Library Store, Inc.
P.O. Box 0964
112 E. South Street
Tremont, IL 61568-0964
www.thelibrarystore.com

Teacher Created Materials, Inc.
6421 Industry Way
Westminster, CA 92683
www.teachercreated.com

Teacher's Friend Publications
A Scholastic Company
Riverside, CA
www2.scholastic.com/browse/teach.jsp

Vernon Library Supplies, Inc.
2851 Cole Court
Norcross, GA 30071
www.vernonlibrarysupplies.com

BOOKS

Burkholder, Kelly. *Puppets*. Vero Beach, FL: Rourke Press, 2001.

Carreiro, Carolyn. *Make Your Own Puppets and Puppet Theaters.* Nashville, TN: Williamson Books, 2005.

Cheyney, Jeanne S. *Big Book of Bulletin Boards for Every Month*. Tucson, AZ: Good Year Book, 2006.

Radcliffe, Loralyn. *Big and Easy Patterns*. Westminster, CA: Teacher Created Materials, Inc., 2004.

Sadler, Wendy. *Puppets*. Chicago, IL: Heinemann Library, 2005.

Sevaly, Karen. *Spring! Idea Book*. Riverside, CA: Teacher's Friend Publications, 2001.

The Best of Mailbox Bulletin Boards, Book 2. Greensboro, NC: Education Center, 2004.

WEBSITES

http://www2.scholastic.com/browse/article.jsp?id=11531

www.ADA.gov

http://childrensbooks.about.com/od/forparents/tp/summer_read
ing.htm

www.kid-cast.com

http://kids.nypl.org/reading/recommended.cfm

http://www.kidsreads.com/lists/classic-lists.asp

INDEX

ABOUT THE AUTHORS

PATRICIA A. MESSNER has been an elementary media specialist for the past 22 years in the Lebanon City School District, Lebanon, Ohio. She earned her Master of Education degree at Miami University, Oxford, Ohio, and her Bachelor's in Elementary Education at Asbury College, Wilmore, Kentucky.

BRENDA S. COPELAND has been an elementary librarian for the past 14 years in the Palmyra School District, Palmyra, Pennsylvania. She earned her Master of Library Science degree at Kutztown University and her Bachelor's in Elementary Education at the University of Delaware.

Brenda and Pat are a sister team who grew up in southwestern Ohio. They have completed this book over the phone and the Internet. Every Sunday afternoon, the world comes to a standstill as Brenda and Pat talk over the week's events and plan the next step, whether it is a section in their book or a story that needs some sparkle.

This dynamic pair loves to dress alike and appear at conferences and book signings. They have appeared in Ohio, Pennsylvania, New Jersey, Oklahoma, and Florida and at ALA and AASL Conferences.

Books written by these authors include *Linking Picture Books to Standards* (Libraries Unlimited, 2003), *Collaborative Library Lessons for the Primary Grades* (Libraries Unlimited, 2004), *Using Picture Books to Teach Language Arts Standards in Grades 3–5* (Libraries Unlimited, 2006), *A Year of Picture Books* (Libraries Unlimited, 2007), and *Everyday Reading Incentives* (Libraries Unlimited, 2009).